20 GREATEST HYMNS

- A Mighty Fortress Is Our God
- All Hail The Power Of Jesus' Name
- Amazing Grace
- Be Thou My Vision
- Blessed Assurance
- Come, Thou Fount of Every Blessing
- Come, Thou Long-Expected Jesus
- He Leadeth Me
- Holy, Holy, Holy
- How Great Thou Art
- It Is Well With My Soul
- Jesus Paid It All
- Jesus Loves Me
- Just As I Am
- Love Divine, All Loves Excelling
- My Hope Is Built On Nothing Less
- O For A Thousand Tongues To Sing
- Rock Of Ages
- To God Be The Glory
- What A Friend We Have In Jesus

ARRANGED BY B. C. DOCKERY

WWW.BENDOCKERY.COM

Copyright © 2022 B. C. Dockery

All rights reserved.

Because this is a single bound book, photocopies are permitted for performance purposes only.

A Mighty Fortress Is Our God

Martin Luther
B. C. Dockery

Arr. ©2022

All Hail the Power of Jesus' Name

Oliver Holden
B. C. Dockery

Arr. ©2022

All Hail the Power of Jesus' Name

Amazing Grace

John Newton

©2022 B C Dockery

Be Thou My Vision

Traditional
B. C. Dockery

Arr. ©2022

Blessed Assurance

Phoebe P. Knapp
B. C. Dockery

Arr. ©2022

Come, Thou Fount of Every Blessing

Traditional
B. C. Dockery

Arr. ©2022

Come, Thou Long-Expected Jesus

Rowland H. Prichard
B. C. Dockery

Arr. ©2022

2 Come, Thou Long-Expected Jesus

He Leadeth Me

William B. Bradbury
B. C. Dockery

Arr. ©2022

Holy, Holy, Holy

John, B. Dykes
arr. B. C. Dockery

©2021

How Great Thou Art

Traditional
B. C. Dockery

Arr. ©2022

Score

It Is Well with My Soul

Philip P. Bliss
B. C. Dockery

Arr. ©2022

Jesus Paid It All

John T. Grape

©2021

Jesus Loves Me

William B. Bradbury

©2020

Jesus Loves Me

Just as I Am

William B. Bradbury
B. C. Dockery

Arr. ©2022

Love Divine, All Loves Excelling

John Zundel
B. C. Dockery

Arr. ©2022

My Hope Is Built On Nothing Less

Score

William B. Bradbury
B. C. Dockery

Arr. ©2022

O for a Thousand Tongues to Sing

Carl G. Glazer
B. C. Dockery

Arr. ©2022

Rock of Ages

Thomas Hastings
B. C. Dockery

Arr. ©2022

To God Be the Glory

William H. Doane
B. C. Dockery

Arr. ©2022

To God Be the Glory

What a Friend We Have in Jesus

Charles C. Converse
B. C. Dockery

Arr. ©2022

A Mighty Fortress Is Our God

Martin Luther
B. C. Dockery

Arr. ©2022

A Mighty Fortress Is Our God

Martin Luther
B. C. Dockery

Arr. ©2022

All Hail the Power of Jesus' Name

Oliver Holden
B. C. Dockery

Arr. ©2022

All Hail the Power of Jesus' Name

Oliver Holden
B. C. Dockery

Arr. ©2022

Amazing Grace

Violin I

John Newton

©2020 B C Dockery

Amazing Grace

Piano

John Newton

©2020 B C Dockery

Be Thou My Vision

Traditional
B. C. Dockery

Arr. ©2022

Be Thou My Vision

Traditional
B. C. Dockery

Arr. ©2022

Blessed Assurance

Phoebe P. Knapp
B. C. Dockery

Violin 1

Arr. ©2022

Blessed Assurance

Phoebe P. Knapp
B. C. Dockery

Piano

Arr. ©2022

Come, Thou Fount of Every Blessing

Traditional
B. C. Dockery

Arr. ©2022

Come, Thou Fount of Every Blessing

Traditional
B. C. Dockery

Arr. ©2022

Come, Thou Long-Expected Jesus

Violin I

Rowland H. Prichard
B. C. Dockery

Arr. ©2022

Come, Thou Long-Expected Jesus

Piano

Rowland H. Prichard
B. C. Dockery

Arr. ©2022

He Leadeth Me

William B. Bradbury
B. C. Dockery

Violin 1

Arr. ©2022

He Leadeth Me

William B. Bradbury
B. C. Dockery

Arr. ©2022

Violin I

Holy, Holy, Holy

John, B. Dykes
arr. B. C. Dockery

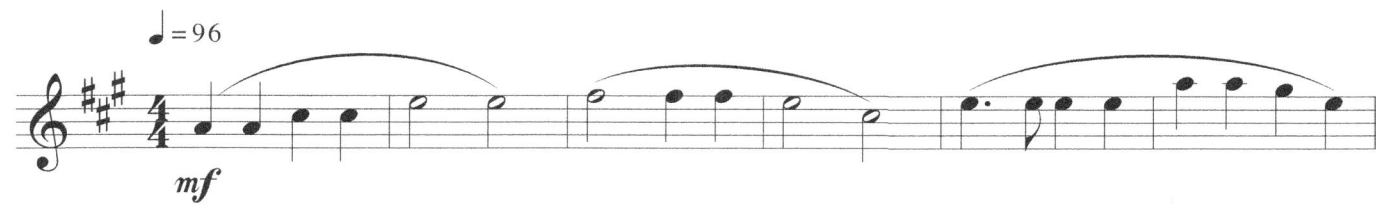
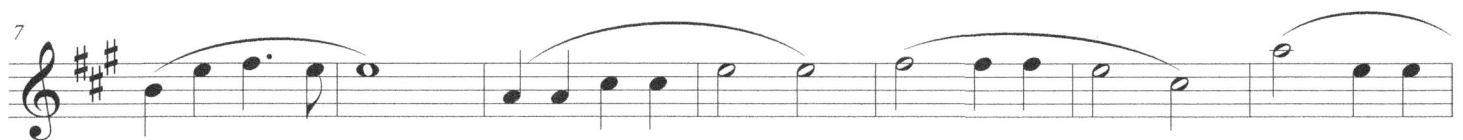
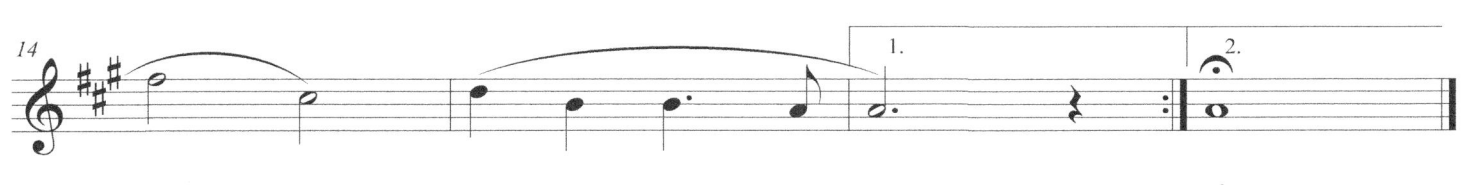

rit.

©2021

Holy, Holy, Holy

Piano

John, B. Dykes
arr. B. C. Dockery

©2021

How Great Thou Art

Violin I

Traditional
B. C. Dockery

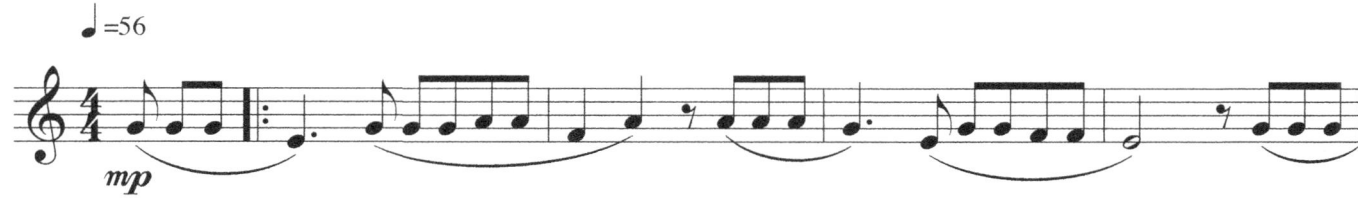

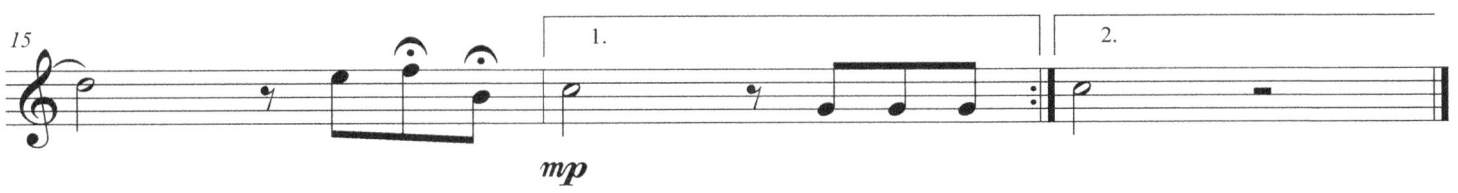

Arr. ©2022

How Great Thou Art

Traditional
B. C. Dockery

Piano

Arr. ©2022

It Is Well with My Soul

Violin I

Philip P. Bliss
B. C. Dockery

Arr. ©2022

It Is Well with My Soul

Piano

Philip P. Bliss
B. C. Dockery

Arr. ©2022

Jesus Paid It All

Violin I

John T. Grape

©2021

Jesus Paid It All

John T. Grape

©2021

Violin I

Jesus Loves Me

William B. Bradbury

Jesus Loves Me

Piano

William B. Bradbury

©2020

Just as I Am

Violin I

William B. Bradbury
B. C. Dockery

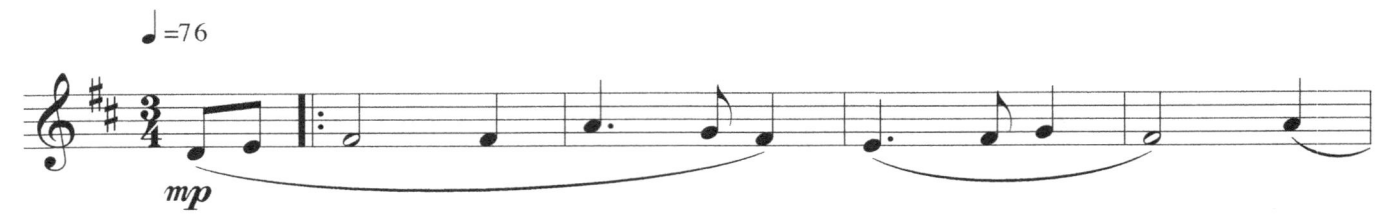

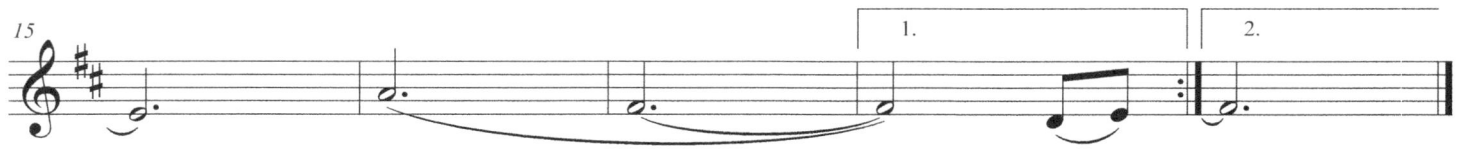

Arr. ©2022

Just as I Am

Piano

William B. Bradbury
B. C. Dockery

Arr. ©2022

Love Divine, All Loves Excelling

Violin I

John Zundel
B. C. Dockery

Arr. ©2022

Love Divine, All Loves Excelling

Piano

John Zundel
B. C. Dockery

Arr. ©2022

Violin I

William B. Bradbury
B. C. Dockery

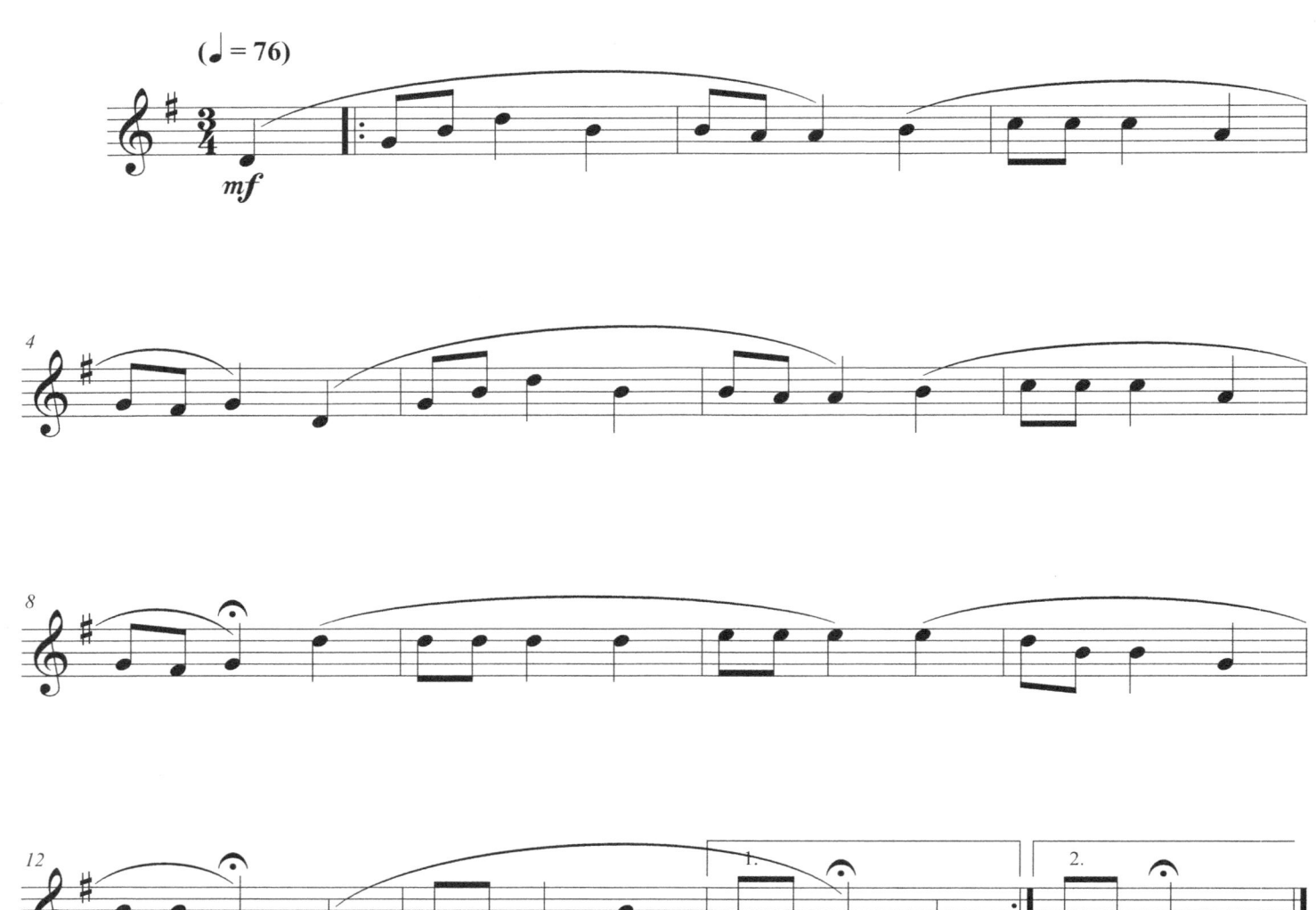

Arr. ©2022

Piano

William B. Bradbury
B. C. Dockery

Arr. ©2022

O for a Thousand Tongues to Sing

Violin I

Carl G. Glazer
B. C. Dockery

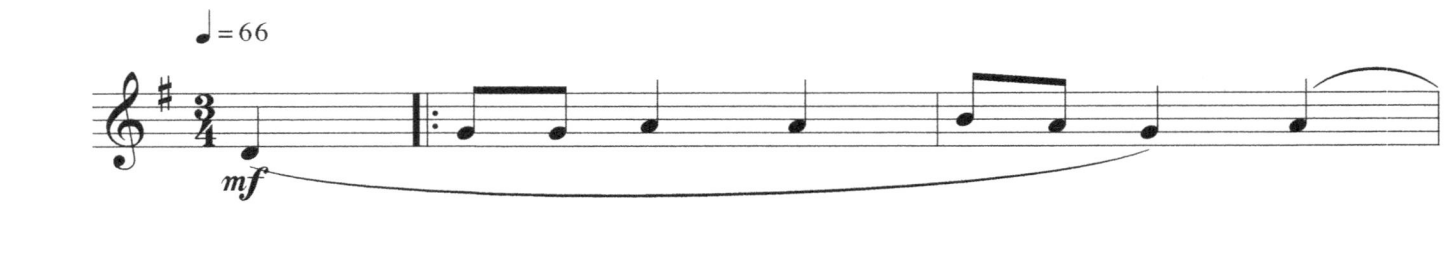

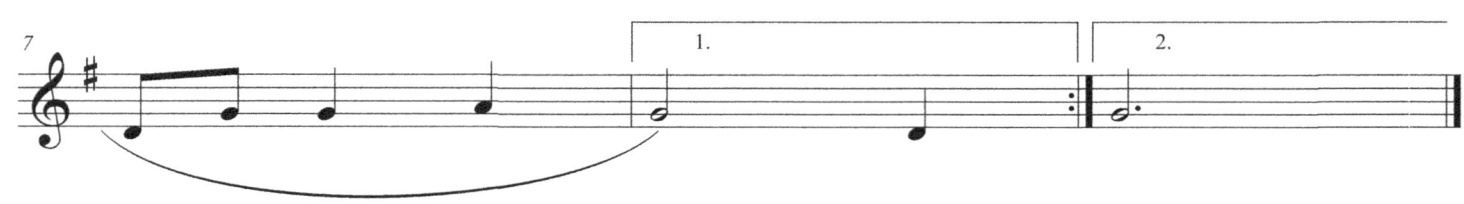

Arr. ©2022

O for a Thousand Tongues to Sing

Piano

Carl G. Glazer
B. C. Dockery

Arr. ©2022

Rock of Ages

Violin I

Thomas Hastings
B. C. Dockery

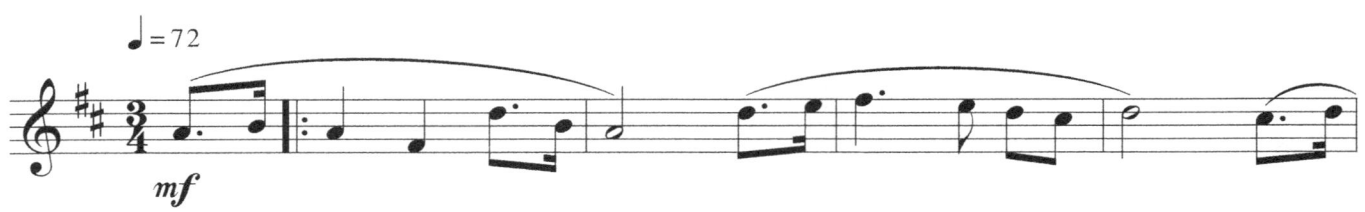

Arr. ©2022

Rock of Ages

Piano

Thomas Hastings
B. C. Dockery

Arr. ©2022

To God Be the Glory

Violin I

William H. Doane
B. C. Dockery

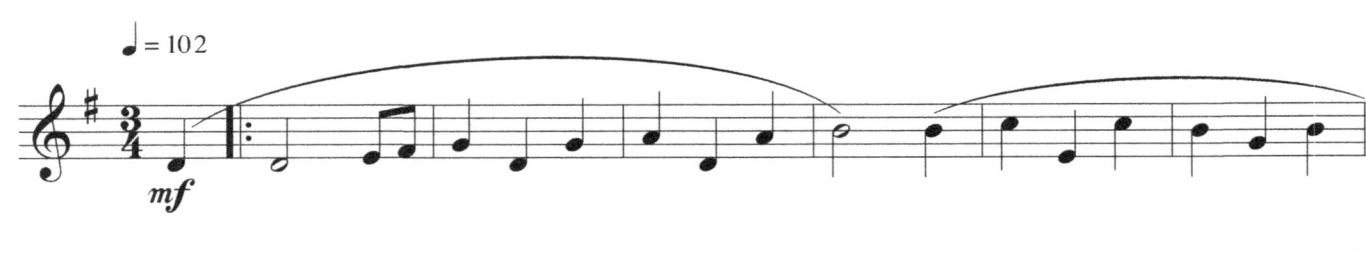

Arr. ©2022

To God Be the Glory

Piano

William H. Doane
B. C. Dockery

Arr. ©2022

What a Friend We Have in Jesus

Violin I

Charles C. Converse
B. C. Dockery

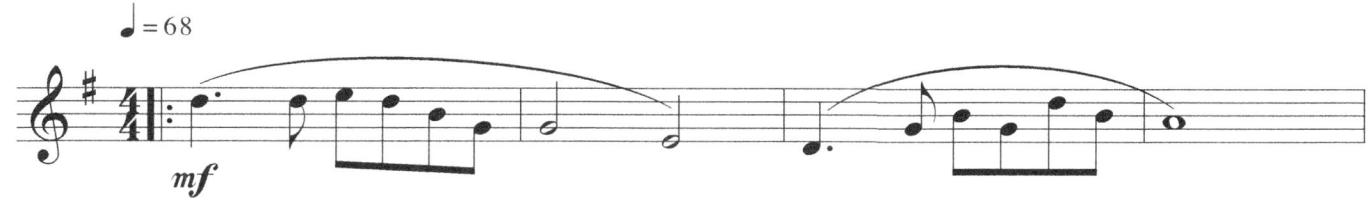

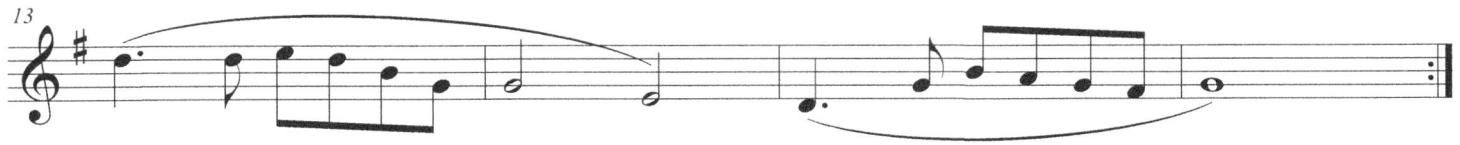

Arr. ©2022

What a Friend We Have in Jesus

Piano

Charles C. Converse
B. C. Dockery

Arr. ©2022

Made in United States
Orlando, FL
24 January 2025